To Hell and Back:
The Power of Forgiveness and Redemption

BY SANDRA GAMBLE

ISBN: 9798681500230

Fire picture purchased on Canva.com
Sky picture, front cover and back cover pictures
belong to the Author.

DEDICATION

This book is dedicated to GOD, who is truly the head of my life. For He gave me the strength to heal so I could help; God allowed me to go through *Hell*, but He walked me back and showed me the *Freedom* in *Forgiveness* and His *Redemptive Power*. Secondly, this book is dedicated to my Mother, Ethel Gamble, who is my hero, my best friend, and my support system in all that I do. I love her to the moon and back.

Lastly, this book is dedicated to everyone that has gone through any type of trauma. It is my hope that after reading this book, it will give you the strength to forgive and help you even further in your journey of emotional freedom.

CONTENTS

ACKNOWLEDGMENTS

I bless your Name God for allowing me to write this book under his divine instructions. Thanks to my Mother Ethel Gamble, my aunt Rosa Gamble, who inspired me to write. I know she is smiling down from Heaven. My aunt, Ruthie Bradley, who has always believed in me. I know she is smiling down from Heaven as well. To all my family and friends that believed in me, and to the people that didn't believe in me I say thank you as well.

Special Acknowledgment to my two big cousins that are actually my brothers Willie Arthur and Verney Bradley thank you for loving me. Special thanks to my cousin, Denise Clegg for taking this journey with me. To the late Corey E. McClintock who meant the world to me may you continue to RIP. To Michael Bolwaire, an awesome young man, who is doing great things that inspired me to push for Greater. I have learned that inspiration can come from anyone. You can tap into somebody's energy, and it can push you higher. The best advice you gave was to keep doing a little bit everyday and to be so good they can't overlook you; also, special thanks to my cousin Cheryl Josey.

My church family Mechanicsville United Methodist Church where I serve as Lay Leader. It was Pastor Patrick Pierre who told me I could write a book because he did! To the Awesome Women of God in my life who inspired me and gave me that extra push Pastor Deedra McLeod, Prophetess Stephanie Mathis, Prophetess Toylinda Smith, Ada Nwankudu and my awesome publisher DeAngela Haynes, who is absolutely a God sent person.

TO HELL AND BACK

You are Dumb! Stupid! Ugly! You will never be anything, you will never amount to anything!! Those were the words spoken to me by my very own father, when I was a small child, I am guessing I must have been around 4 or 5 years old. I can recall these awful words so vividly coming out of my Father's mouth. As a small child, I was confused, overwhelmed, alarmed, my little mind could not or would not allow me to understand why such hurtful words were coming from the mouth of my own Father towards me.

Aren't parents supposed to love you? Aren't parents supposed to provide for you, aren't parents supposed to be loving, caring, and kind towards their children? Should parents protect you from pain, hurt, and the harsh realities of life, especially if you are a little girl whose is made of Sugar and spice and everything nice. This was not my reality, the first pain, the first hurt, the first trauma was invoked upon me from inside my home, by my Biological Father.

My self-esteem was shattered, myself-worth and self-acceptance was non-existent. In that very moment I knew something was wrong with me. After all, this is my Father and if he said something is wrong with me, surely it had to be true, and if he couldn't see good in me, then surely I wasn't good. I was broken, defective, and malfunctioned. Not only was I malfunctioned on the outside, I was malfunctioned on the inside.

When I looked into the mirror, I saw an ugly little girl, unaccepted of oneself, someone fractured. My Father did not like me, I later understood many years later that he did not like himself. He shared with me how he did not want me! His very words to me was I told your mother to get rid of you! I wanted a son. I even remember him telling me that he struck my mother in her stomach when she was pregnant with me in hopes of her having a miscarriage. Many years later, I asked Mother about this story and she confirmed that it was true. BUT GOD!!!

Jeremiah 29:11 says, "For I know the plans I have for you, declares the LORD, plans to prosper you and not to harm you, plans to give you hope and a future."

Even before I knew it, even before I understood it, GOD had plans for me! And what the enemy meant for harm, God turned it around for my good! I have learned that the Enemy doesn't care who he uses in an attempt to abort the promises of GOD. He will even use the people closest to you and in my case, this was my Father in an effort to make you miss your destiny. Often, the enemy gets a glimpse of your future and he does everything he can to derail you from reaching that expectant end.

I entered this world on November 15th; my Mother's due date was the middle of January. I entered this world Mother recalls kicking and screaming at 4lbs and 12 ounces. I came into this world fighting. With underdeveloped lungs and a compromised immune system for being 8 weeks early; Mom reports I made progress and came home quicker than anyone expected. Living with my father was very unpredictable, there was always tension, and unrest in our home.

My mother and I never knew from day to day or sometimes minute to minute what the day would bring, or what would set him off. To the outside world, we were the perfect little family. My parents both worked and were able to purchase their own home in the early 70s; we had a perfectly manicured yard, we dressed up and we went to church on Sundays as a family. My Father held positions in the church, was over organizations and worked at DuPont.

However, behind closed doors we were literally living a lie, a nightmare where my mother and I lived in fear and intimidation, put downs and let downs, verbal and physical altercations, were the norm in my house. My Father would target me in an effort to get Mother upset because he knew if he started with me, she would intervene. My Mother always tried to protect me; however I later understood that she was a victim herself.

So many memories that used to haunt me, but one in particular stood out to me, being when he got mad with

Mother because she wouldn't conform to his unrealistic demands. He became very angry, called me over to him and proceeded to light my right ponytail with his cigarette lighter and singed my hair. For many years, I could smell that scorch smell in my nose although it was no longer happening.

This was Post-Traumatic stress disorder, but God took it away in time. The time when he would drink his tea and actually spit in his tea and make me drink it, or the time where he made me suck his big toe. All these situations resulted in verbal and physical altercations between him and mother; most of the time he would beat her badly. He would especially go for her face, telling her no one wanted her, and that she was ugly. My mother hid her abuse from friends and family never telling anyone that we were prisoners in our own home; sleeping with the enemy.

My Father was very controlling and infidelity was a normal in our home. The lack of respect for his wife and child was evident; he would say things to Mother like, "I pay bills, so I have a right to have another woman or other women," or he would tell Mother, "You don't have the right to question me." My Father most definitely had a sense of entitlement. At times, his verbal abuse was harsh, and I can remember him telling Mother, "You are ugly nobody else is going to want you."

He would call her out of her name, degrading her. I couldn't understand this behavior. I would actually see mother looking in the mirror and agreeing with what my dad said about her, and I can also remember comforting mother telling her how beautiful she was, and I was happy that she was my mother. Mother always tried to make up for my Father bad behavior. I think she felt bad that she chose him to be my Father.

I also believed that Mother didn't take time to know my Father very well because she was in a toxic environment where her parents drank and fought and she was ready to leave home, so she traded one bad situation for another, people in pain tend to attract pain. I can remember having a beautiful pink and white room with a Canopy bed, the room was fit for a Princess.

I had a singing jewelry box, I had my very own room, after all I was an only child; however although my room was decorated for a princess. I definitely didn't feel like a princess. Actually, I felt like an ugly duckling. I couldn't properly enjoy my bedroom due to the unrest that was in my house. For I never knew when I would have to run to the neighbors for help. I remember once, my father was fighting my mother, and it got so violent until I jumped out of my bedroom window and rode my bike to the neighbor's house for help.

In those moments, I felt so helpless. My neighbor intervened and talked with my father about his behavior that night, and that night the fighting ceased after the conversation. I can remember crying myself to sleep that night. Another vivid memory I have from my childhood is when I wanted a baby alive. This was a new doll that had come on the scene, it was popular and a must have toy. I can remember expressing my desire for a baby alive.

I begged and pleaded with Mother to consider getting this doll for me, and I knew If I had any chance of getting the doll, it had to have come from her because my Father wouldn't buy it. For whatever reason, I still remember how much Mother paid for my baby alive $27, and it may not seem like much money today. However, this was a huge sacrifice in the 70's. I was so in love with my doll, she could blink her eyes, cry, suck a bottle, urinate and I would have to change her diaper; for a little while I was a very happy child.

This was until my Father came home one evening and started with Mother. I can remember vividly playing on the floor in the living room with my doll, trying to ignore the yelling and screaming; when he walked towards me and ripped my doll out of my arms. I cried desperately begging my father to return the doll back to me, where it belonged.

He just chuckled, as if he was getting pleasure out of causing me pain. I ran behind my Father pleading with him to return my doll, all of my cries and pleads fell on deaf ears. My Father was 6 feet weighing around 185lbs. I guess I was around 6 or 7 years of age when this incident occurred. My Father proceeded to go into the kitchen and get a knife. He then dismembered my doll at the neck, and I felt as if I had died inside. I was crying and tugging at my Father so hard pleading with him, asking him why he would do that. He proceeded to go to the wooden heater, open up the heater and threw my dismembered doll into the heater; my world was shattered.

I felt as if my little heart was going to come out of my chest, and to make matters worse, my father appeared to be enjoying every moment of this, laughing loudly as I sobbed uncontrollably. I can remember trying to grab him around the leg and he pushed me to the floor, needless to say this was a bad night in the Gamble household.

I can remember crying myself to sleep that night, trying to understand why so much pain from inside my home, why did my Father hate me so much and why won't mother leave, I had many sleepless nights in that home, I was a very depressed child, although I didn't know what depression was , looking back I'm sure that I was depressed. I thought about running away but where would I go? Why was I stuck? Why was I being punished? What did I do to deserve this?

And honestly I thought about ending my Father's life or even my own just to end the pain, I never acted on it, but I actually thought about it. I was betrayed by the very people that were supposed to take care of me; momma failed to protect me because she wouldn't leave, or kept going back, and my father failed me because he was the person inflicting the pain.

I felt like a hamster on a wheel that could not get off. I felt like an imposter; to the outside world I had everything by society's standards, but I actually had nothing. I would put on a big smile when I went to school because I didn't want anyone to know about my home life. I managed to get good grades in school, even though I was under tremendous pressure at home. Nothing was ever good enough in my Father's eyes, and I spent so many years trying to be good for him; to get him to acknowledge me. If I made a B, it wasn't good enough and if I made A's it was minimized. I grew up uncertain, unsure of myself.

If I washed dishes, he would find or say there was a spot, and I would have to rewash them. If I cooked, he would say the food wasn't seasoned properly or the food wasn't done. I could never do good in my Father's eyes. Another memory I have is when one night, he went into a rage and made Mother and I get in the car; I guess I was around 7 or 8.

He was driving at a high speed, and he said he was going to kill us. He said he was going to not stop at the stop sign and run us into the woods; I surely thought I was going to die. Somehow and somewhere, he did stop at the stop sign. It was a sigh of relief, God had spared us. Another memory I have is when he threatened to kill us once again, but Mother and I got out of the house. I can remember us lying down in a cool ditch to hide from my father to keep him from harming us. When he cooled down and left home that night, we snuck back into the house and mom made a pallet in the closet; she and I both slept there all night long in hopes of him not finding us.

I learned to be very still and not make noise. I am going to tell you women, staying in an abusive relationship negatively impacts your child or children's emotional well-being. They learn how to mask their pain, and it leaves them fearful and uncertain. If you cannot find the strength to leave for yourself, please find the strength to leave for your children. The abuse started to impact me; my behavior changed.

I no longer cared about academics; although I was a good student. I hated my Father, and I was angry at my Mother. Plain and simple, these two had failed me big time. "Why was I even born," I asked myself this question? After years of mother going back and forth, leaving and returning, because of his empty promises to change, only to find out when she returned, that it was more of the same.

The put down, the letdown, the ridicule, the disrespect, the infidelity, the blows ups, the aggression and more of the same. At school I had peers talking about what they did with their father on the weekends, such as going to get ice-cream, or their father taking them to the movies, and I can remember lying to my peers about what my father and I did on weekends. I was too embarrassed or ashamed to let people know my truth.

My truth was my father and I did nothing together; he rarely spent time with me, and it was almost as if he was in the house with us, but emotionally not available for us. A few times, he did take me with him to his job where he would pick up his check on Wednesday; I enjoyed going with my father. This was our little time together; keep in mind, I was always trying to meet his approval in some way or another.

I can remember specifically this particular Wednesday, he took me with him to pick up his check. I was thinking, "Maybe I will get an ice cream cone; maybe he will be nice to me today." I had high hopes; I guess I was about 7 years of age. I remember him picking up his check, and I also remember him driving to another location, to meet a woman and a little boy. I saw them chatting, and they proceeded to come to my side, and he introduced me to this woman and her small son.

He told me her name, he said this is my friend, and I immediately didn't feel right. I don't know if it was the way he said it or how they looked at each other, but I knew this wasn't no ordinary friend. I kept saying to myself this lady's name sounds familiar. Why do I know it, and why would he take me to meet her? As they departed, they hugged, and he kissed her on the lips. I knew this was wrong. To this day, I can remember that the lady wore a nice pair of slacks, a fitted blouse with a scarf tied around her neck and big sunglasses. When I got back home and was alone with Mother, I then told her about my encounter with this mystery woman.

My mother asked me her name and I told her, she became very angry and upset. That night when my father returned home, my mother confronted him about taking me to meet his mistress. Mother knew exactly who she was, and actually I knew who she was also without knowing. This was the lady that would call our house and ask me to speak to my father, now it all made sense,

As a result of mother confronting him, an altercation broke out, and I got confronted by my father for telling mother about his encounter; this resulted in me being slapped to the floor, and I was also told that I would never go with him again when he picked up his check. Once again, I managed to do something wrong, without knowing that I didn't do anything wrong. I was just an innocent kid caught up in an unhealthy toxic environment.

I was convinced that if my parents didn't get away from each other, one of them would eventually kill the other. Another memory I had was when my father decided to take us on a family vacation to Six Flags Over Georgia. I was so excited because he never did anything with us; after all, I was always seeking the approval of my Father, although I never got it. We drove to Six Flags Over Georgia and slept in the rest area after my Father refused to get us a room.

I remember being so tired from sleeping in the car. My mother and I had to wash up in the rest area's restroom; despite my Father having a pocket full of money that he freely showed us. I can remember the sad look on my mother's face. She actually had to fix my hair on the trolley as we rode into the Amusement Park. Again, I couldn't understand why my father hated us; especially me so much. Again, this confirmed all over again that something was surely wrong with me.

My Father was very controlling towards my mother, he would not allow her to have friends over, and he didn't like when she visited her family. He would clock the miles in the car to see how far we would drive. Another memory that I had is when my mother, aunt and I attended a Gospel concert at Riley Ball Park; I must have been around 8 or 9. We saw The 5 Blind Boys, Tommy Ellison, and some other Gospel singers; we had a wonderful time, worshiping and singing alone with the groups.

I always loved listening to Gospel music and attending events with my favorite aunt Ruthie, but when my aunt bought us back home, as we entered through the back door into the den, my Father instantly attacked my mother, pulling all of her clothes off, and violently hitting her. I stood there numb, once again trying to figure out what had happened. How could it be wrong to go to a Gospel Singing and praise and serve God, and why was this happening; will I lose my mother tonight to violence?

My mother fought back, but she was no match for my father, I finally remember running into the living room and grabbing a lamp, and I struck my father across the head to get him off of Mother. I was terrified, but I had to do something. He stopped fighting her, and he sat on the floor gagging as if he was going to throw up. He had a cut on the side of his head from where I hit him, and I knew for sure he was going to kill me when he came to himself, but he didn't. Later on, when he gathered himself and went to bed.

I helped Mother clean herself up, she had so many bruises especially on her face; her beautiful face was unrecognizable, in that moment. I hated father even more, I loved my father, but I hated him. I couldn't understand who he was and why he was the way he was. I grew up in church singing on the SunBeam Choir, going to Sunday School, and participating on Easter Sunday.

I knew that the Bible said Honor thy Mother and thy Father so thy days may be long upon the land, but how do you honor a father who does not deserve to be honored? How do you honor a Father who dishonors you, who is supposed to love, protect, and adore you, but has been the source of all your pain? Again I went to bed angry, hurt, sad, lonely, confused; every emotion to have I had so many other nights.

I began to wish my Father would die, just leave, get into a car accident, or I would wonder how to harm him without getting caught but then, I would feel guilty for having those thoughts. Surely, God wasn't pleased with me, but where was God in all of this? Is He real? Am I being punished? Is there something I did to deserve this kind of Father? After more years of leaving and returning, when I turned 13, I finally said to Mother that I was tired of this life. I told her that my grades were dropping, and I no longer cared. I explained to her that I didn't care about having my own room, nor did I care about this beautiful house that we had no peace in.

I explained to her that I wasn't happy nor was I ever happy. All I wanted was peace for once; I asked her to leave at that moment. She made the decision to leave and not return. She had found the courage to leave. I asked her to promise me that this was it, and she did. Needless to say, this was the happiest day of my life. My mother and I packed up what we could, her nephew came to pick us up, and we left.

Mother left all her possessions other than clothes because my Father would not allow her to take anything, as we drove off, he said, I am glad you two are going! So, I can entertain who I want to entertain and have my lady friends over. Sometimes, parents believe they are doing their children a favor by staying with their spouse, but in actuality it harms the children emotionally for the children see the constant turmoil. They see the living ongoing hell, and they witness the horror.

I had a front row set to the horror movie that was playing in my house. The Monster was my Father and the Victim was my mother and myself. My mother and I left a 3-bedroom fully furnished home with many commodities, to move in with her brother in a trailer, at a trailer park, where we had to share a bedroom.

This was the happiest I had ever been, sharing a bedroom with my mother at the age of 13; although I didn't have my own room, what I did have was a peace of mind, something I had never had in a long time; if ever. I have learned that material things don't matter when you have no happiness and peace. Over the years, I have learned that peace at any price is no peace at all, and I have also learned that material things mean absolutely nothing if you aren't happy and don't have peace. My mother and I for so many years, never knew what peace was until now.

We stayed with my Uncle for about a year until we moved into our own apartment, this is when Mother filed for divorce. The day of the divorce hearing, mom and I arrived, my Father and his girlfriend, who happens to be the woman he introduced me too many years ago arrived, my aunt and grandmother were there as well. The judge asked me who I wanted to live with as I was of age, and I expressed to the Judge that my desire was to continue to live with my Mother.

I was sure my Father wouldn't contest this; after all he never had time for me even when we were under the same roof. My Father wanted the house and Mother didn't contest it; although I'm sure if she would have provided information to the judge about all his infidelities over the years, she would have easily been awarded the house as well as alimony. The judge ordered my father to be responsible for all of my clothes for both school and church, and he would also be responsible for my college tuition and was ordered to pay child support; after all he made substantially more money than Mother.

Although it appeared that everything was okay and everyone agreed, I knew that it would not be okay at least for me. My Father wasn't happy about having to pay child support. After the proceedings, the telephone calls started. He would call and say things to me like, "Tell your mother I will not pay child support to her for her for another man to spend my money!"

He would pick me up from school and harass me about telling my mother to drop child support. He would yell and scream at me demanding that I make Mother drop the support; my nerves were wrecked!! I had a lot of anxiety and fears even as a teenager. I feared my Father and what he might do, so I asked myself when does this end and if there is a God why want you intervene? I can remember becoming angry and bitter towards my Father, praying at times that he would die and then feeling bad for praying and hoping this. After all the Bible says honor thy mother and thy father so thy days will be long along the land.

I knew God was somewhere just not close enough to my circumstances or situation. I thought, "Why did God abandon me when I needed him the most?" Finally, after being harassed on multiple occasions by my Father for the past several months, Mother agreed to drop the child support. Over my teen years, I started to act out some, becoming somewhat rebellious and angry and promiscuous at times.

I guess I was buying into the words spoken over my life by my Father, "You are dumb, stupid, ugly, you will never be anything, you will never amount to anything," but even in my wilding ways, I somehow felt as if God had a bigger plan for my life; I just didn't know how to figure it out on my own. I attended church, I sang on the Sun-beam and the Junior Choir, I went to Sunday School, and I was an active member in church, but I was still so full of hurt, pain, and anger. I guess I was looking for love in all the wrong places and as a result, I became sexually active as a teenager. I thought that I was drawn to older boys, but what I was looking for was a Father figure.

I come to understand that unresolved childhood issues result in repeated actions, or unhealthy relationships with self and others. Though I was acting out some, I did manage to keep decent grades and graduated from high school with honors. Although my Father had his ways, he was interested in my academics and did visit the school frequently over my school years to talk with my teachers and show interest in my school work.

This was a positive and it did make the difference. By the time I graduated from high school at the age of 18, I was involved with a man that was 24 years of age. He had a lot of the characteristics that my Father had; he was controlling, verbally abusive, jealous, and a womanizer. What we don't address, we are subject to repeat; to parents, children mostly live what they learn.

The first man a girl learns how to love is her Father and if this relationship is somehow unhealthy or toxic, she does not have the proper blueprint to gauge what real love looks like. To the women reading this book, I beg of you to choose a mate for your children that can show your daughters that they are Queens and that they are deserving of real, happy, healthy, God-ordained love.

I spent 7 years in this unhealthy relationship that did not add value to me, my self-esteem or self-worth in any way. In fact, it kept me believing that this was all I had deserved. When I went to college in August of 1989, I did not know what I wanted to major in. All I knew was when I graduated from College, I was determined to go far away from my Father. I was finally free of him or so I thought.

When I first got to college, my Mother and Aunt took me. This was my first time being away from home, and it was a culture shock to say the least. However, I met some great friends my freshman year, and I'm happy to report that we are still friends. My freshman year, I put down for my major Accounting; although I had no clue in what I wanted to do in my life.

I had taken it in high school at the Vocational School and was told you could make really good money in that field. I excelled during my Freshman year, however by my Sophomore year, I was beginning to take classes within my major and I absolutely hated it. I knew I had made a mistake, but I didn't know how to get out of it. This was until we had a career placement test, and I took it. The Instructor came to me and said, "Ms. SANDRA GAMBLE, you may want to consider changing your major. According to this career test, you should be in the Human Services/Social Work field." I was delighted that it was not all in my head and without a second thought, I changed my major my second semester year to Psychology.

This was it for me!! I could now try and understand why my Father behaved the way that he did towards me. I was looking for answers, I thrived in Psychology because I needed to make sense of things that did not make sense. Although I was learning about the human mind and how it works, Abnormal Psychology, it did not excuse or erase the pain of the past and my childhood wounds and memories.

I was still angry, I was still hurting, and I was still confused. May 8, 1994 on Mother's Day Sunday, I graduated from South Carolina State University with my Bachelor of Science Psychology; as my family looked on, I walked across that stage, obtaining my degree. Being the first grandchild to graduate from College, I was full of mixed emotions, unsure and uncertain about the future, but what I knew for sure that I would never live in South Carolina again; at least that is what I believed. My family was so proud of me that Sunday, and I was showered with gifts. The only person that didn't say they were proud, was my dad.

I thought that I could move forward with my life, but GOD had other plans. One month after I came out of college, my Father got sick at work, and he was placed on medical leave and ended up in the hospital for several days for depression. I was thinking, "He will be back to his old self in no time, and I can go on with my life." I was planning to move to Atlanta with my best friend Denise. She had already made the move.

Shortly after the first hospitalization, he had another hospitalization for depression, and the doctors said he had a nervous breakdown. I became angry because he wasn't getting better, and this might mean a delay in my plans. I told myself he better get better quickly because I'm not going to abort my plans. He didn't take care of me when I needed him, and I'm certainly not going to take care of him. Fast forward 12 years, and what began as one hospitalization, ended up being 32 hospitalizations; some for mental illness others for health issues.

His diagnosis changed from Depression to Bipolar Manic-Depressive Disorder with Psychotic Features. In other words, the moods range from Depressive to Manic, both episodes put him in crisis. When he was depressed, he was suicidal, he had lost interest, increased need for sleep, lack of self-care and weight loss. This normally required hospitalization, and when he was experiencing manic episodes, he made high risk decisions such as spending money excessively.

Believing he was rich, inflated ego, decreased need for sleep, increased drinking and driving, increased energy, escape from reality, and low impulse control. Although he was self-destructive, he didn't see it and actually enjoyed the high of the manic episode.

When he was depressed, he willingly sought hospitalization when he was manic. I had to force hospitalization through involuntary commitment papers. This process left me looking like the bad person, because it resulted in him being picked up by the Police and taken to the hospital for an evaluation.

This most likely would result in him staying in the hospital for several days up until 2 weeks to get regulated on medications. Of course, this made me look like the villain even the more. Let's talk about the next 12 years from 1994 until 2006. We often talk about the woman with the issue of blood that had issues for 12 years. Until she had an encounter with Jesus and she touched him, virtue went out of him, and instantly she was healed.

I can relate to this twelve years of dealing with my Father; what I thought would be several months turned out to be 12 years. Over these 12 years, I'm going to be transparent and tell you that I didn't do everything right, nor was I happy about the place that I felt God had me at, and yet again I felt as if I was being punished. Why am I having to take care of a Father that didn't take care of me?

How is this fair, why can't I be rid of this man, and why did Mother choose this man to be my Father? I was so angry for so long, at God, at myself, at Mother and at life. I was saying to God, "He robbed me of my childhood and now he is going to rob me of my adulthood. What about me God?" There were times when I even questioned if there was a God although I knew that it was. How could the all-seeing, all-knowing, all-loving God, allow his daughter to continue to suffer? Or what I saw as suffering.

I felt abandoned as if I was an orphan, and I had very little support and help as it pertains to my Father. It was basically as if the family said you went to school for this, this is your Daddy, it's your problem and you deal with it; I felt so alone. What I have learned is that oftentimes, people run away from what they don't understand, and my family, like so many families, didn't understand, nor did they want to understand. What was sent to break me actually made me, through my pain and suffering, I found a real relationship with Jesus Christ!

No one told me about Jesus, I had my own personal encounter. It wasn't God sent, but it was God used! Even though I understood mental illness, the pain that my Father inflicted upon me was very real. In these 12 years of my caring for my Father, I spent most of them angry and resentful.

I was bitter, I partied excessively and drank during my 20's. My Father never took responsibility for his emotional health, but he never accepted the fact that he had a mental illness. This resulted in a lot of unnecessary hospitalizations, and one time when he was in crisis and became manic, he thought he was rich. He gave all of his clothes away, and started mailing various women $500 checks. I was running around trying to stop payment on those checks, and he had a lot of people take advantage of him during this time.

I can remember him being very paranoid and believing that the FBI was watching him; this particular time he wouldn't allow me in his house, because he thought that the FBI had me bugged. My Father became so aggressive, paranoid, and erratic in his behavior. He was calling the white house, and I can remember an CIA agent came to visit me in reference to my father.

I can remember times when he would go into stores and expose himself, and people would come back and tell me. I was so embarrassed at his actions and behaviors. There were times when he believed he was being followed by the FBI, and he got into a car accident that landed him in Jail for DUI. Another time I was actually working in a social club as a bar-tender, and he came into the club that night. He came over to me and told me that the CIA and FBI were in the Social club, and he demanded that I get down on the floor and get down now. I tried to reason with him, and he became belligerent and said he had a gun. When I got down on the floor, he started running and left the club.

I later got a call that he was locked up for DUI in Kershaw County, so his best friend and I got him out of jail that Sunday morning. That Monday morning I was at the Mental Health Center signing involuntary commitment papers for him to go into the hospital because his actions made him a danger to himself and others. Of course, he was very upset with me for doing this; after all it wasn't anything wrong with him.

December 2002, I was at work when I received a call that my father was involved in yet again another car accident where he had total-lossed his Ford Explorer after only having it for 3 days. He was airlifted to Richland memorial hospital, and when I got to the hospital, I was told that he had fractured a bone in his neck and it would require surgery. New Year's Eve, my aunt and I sat in the waiting area while my father and her brother had surgery to repair the fracture in his neck.

This was a good opportunity to inquire to my aunt about my father and how he was as a child. Her response, "Your Father has always had something wrong with him, Sandra." She said for the longest time, he had tried to get her to drink poison when they were children. Now, things were making sense; my dad had mental illness even as a child. She shared with me that his behavior was always strange. People back then, didn't get help for mental illness. As a race and a culture, we have to get to a place in the Black community where we have to talk about mental illness and stop making it a stigma. It isn't a character flaw, or a fall from grace, nor a lack of faith.

It is real just as hypertension and cancer have progressions and when left untreated, it can be deadly. Mental illness is treatable and people can get better when managed properly. Six hours later, he came out of surgery, and God graced him with grace, as the surgery went well; he wasn't paralyzed. I have learned that GOD never stops extending His grace, love and mercy towards us even when we are far away from His will.

After surgery, my father spent the next several weeks in rehab, he was released from the hospital after spending over 3 weeks in the hospital. He was to continue in home physical therapy; however after a few short days he stopped the Physical therapist from coming out. About 6 or 7 weeks later, after getting home from the neck injury, as still having issues with his neck due to the neck fusion and the lack of range of motion, he convinced his former co-worker and friend to take him to purchase another Ford Explorer without me knowing. One afternoon, I heard a car in my yard and when I looked outside, I saw that it was my Father in another Ford Explorer.

In that moment my heart sunk, I told him that he should have waited until he healed, his response was, "I'm the parent and you are the child." He sped out of the yard, I had an awful feeling, I immediately started to pray. Fast forward several days later on a Saturday morning in March, I was driving to my kickboxing class when I was stopped by the wife of a local Garage worker, who asked me how my father was doing.

My response, he is okay still healing from the accident. There was a quietness, and she said to me, "Sandra, your father was involved in a car accident late last night." She said, "We tried to reach you, but the line kept being busy." She said, "He totally lost his truck on his way home," and she shared she didn't know how bad it was, but from the looks of it, it was pretty bad. I was stunned, speechless, I couldn't believe what I was hearing. I thank her for letting me know and told her that I would check on him at McLeod hospital. I never made it to kickboxing class that day, and I returned home to inform my mother what I just found out.

I sat on her bed stunned, afraid to call the hospital unsure what I would hear. Due to HIPAA laws, they couldn't give me any information about his condition other than that he was there. An hour or so later, I got myself together enough to drive over to the hospital; Mother came along with me. It was a quiet ride over, when I entered the room, the first thing my Father asked was I upset; UPSET was an understatement.

He said, "Sandra, don't be mad, you told me not to get another vehicle." My response to him was that you don't understand how your decisions negatively impact me, and how he was selfish how he made decisions, and I also told him how he was irresponsible in how he manages his mental health. No response from him. I later found out that he had crushed the ball and socket in his hip requiring yet another surgery, and he had also broken his collarbone; despite his accident, he was blessed considering how bad it could have been.

From these injuries, he stayed in the hospital from March until the middle of May that year; a combined hospital and rehab stay of 3 to 4 months, and yours truly had the task of working full-time and spending time at the hospital. My father wouldn't comply with rehab and as a result was never able to walk without the assistance of the walker. I was burned out and at my wits end.

I could remember crawling in my aunt's bed tired, tearful and overwhelmed; this was Friday, September 22nd, I asked her when does it end? She was a woman of strong faith who loved God, and she helped nurture my relationship with God. I can remember watching Billy Graham with her when I was a child, "Her response to me was that the Lord has His set time for all things and when he says that's it then that will be it. On Monday September 25, 2006, 32 hospitalizations later, my Father walked out on his porch and had a massive heart attack and just like that it was over. A neighbor passed by and saw him on the porch and called the Paramedics.

My aunt Rosa, the very one I had the conversation with on Friday, called me and shared with me that my Father had gotten sick, and they transported him to the hospital. Her response, check on your Father. I don't know how bad it is. I drove to the hospital thinking that it would be like it always would, he would go in for a breathing treatment, stay a few days and come back home. My Father had a lot of health issues especially with his lungs as he was a longtime smoker.

When I arrived at the Emergency Room, I was approached by Verna Moore who introduced herself as the

Coroner. She said to me are you next of kin to Johnny Gamble, my response was yes, and I had gone to the hospital alone. She went on to say that your father didn't have any identification on him, however the nurses and doctors recognize him from him frequenting the hospital. Sorry to inform you that he didn't make it. It appears he had a massive heart attack and was probably deceased before he hit the floor. I was stunned, she says I need you to ID him. At that moment, my head was spinning.

I felt as if I was in a movie, I told myself maybe this is a case of mistaken identity; however when I turned the corner to the room, I saw his feet and I knew without a shadow of a doubt that it was him. I sit quietly in the room processing my life, the last 12 years, this moment, saddened that he was gone, but happy that I forgave him completely. I rub his forehead, and he was still warm to the touch.

He looked so peaceful as if all of his worries and pain was over. I saw my Father age disappear from his face, and I said to myself, maybe he found peace in death because it seemed as if he couldn't find it in life. I started to make calls to family to let them know what had happened. September 30th 2006, I laid my Father to rest. What I have learned through this journey of to hell and back, was the power of forgiveness and redemption. What do I hope you have learned from reading this? I have learned that GOD is so real, that He met me when I was at my worst, and He accepted me and loved me right where I was at. I learned that although my father may not have been able to love me the way I needed, he loved me the way that he could.

I learned that God is truly a healer, not only is He a healer in our physical body, but He is also a healer in our emotional places; all we have to do is surrender it to Him. I learned that I forgave my Father in pieces and that's okay because forgiveness is a process, but well worth the journey! I have learned that you owe it to yourself to heal so you can help, and that you are responsible for your healing; even though you may not have been responsible for your hurt.

I have learned that forgiveness is for you and while it doesn't excuse the behaviors of the ones that hurts you, it releases you of the grip and bondage that once held you. Unforgiveness erodes your soul; it's like drinking poison and waiting for the other person to die. When left unchecked, unforgiveness will and can stop you from forming healthy, lasting relationships. I walked out of *Unforgiveness Prison*, and the person that got free was me. It allowed me to move from a place of *Victim to Victory*! It allowed me to change the narrative and the story that I told myself. While I don't necessarily like this journey, if I had to do it all over again I would, because although it may not have been God sent, it was surely God used.

I have a real relationship with my Heavenly Father; not religion. I'm a sum total of my experiences, as this experience has made me a better person, a better counselor, a better friend, a better daughter, and a better child of GOD. It is my prayer that I showed my father what my Heavenly Father shows us; Unconditional Love.

No longer do I believe that I'm all negative things that my earthly father called me.

I'm An Overcomer, A Purpose Pusher, A World Changer, fearfully and wonderfully made, created on purpose with purpose, and the apple of God's eye. I'm a King's kid with heavenly benefits. I may not have done the test perfectly, but I stayed for the test and God rewards obedience. Only God could turn my pain into purpose, and the very thing that was sent to destroy me, thrusted me into my destiny. I was once the woman with the issue with Dad, but GOD! I touched the Him within the hem and I was made well!!

The journey to forgiveness isn't easy, but its doable; you are already in pain, so make it pay, it will be well worth it. I pray that the persons reading this book will find the strength and the courage to fight for freedom. My Master Coach told me that *Champions Do the Work*!! You are all champions, so let's do the work. May you find the strength to forgive all that have hurt you, and may you find strength to forgive yourself if need be. May the love, grace, provision and protection of GOD bless you abundantly.

ABOUT THE AUTHOR

Sandra Gamble is a Native of Lee County, Bishopville, S.C. She is a 1989 High School Graduate of Mount Pleasant High School. A 1994 graduate of South Carolina State University with a Bachelor's of Science Degree in Psychology, and a 2006 Honor Graduate of Webster University with a Master of Arts in Counseling with an Emphasis in Mental Health.

Sandra is the proud daughter of Ethel Gamble and the Late Johnny Gamble. She is a Certified Life Coach, Motivational Speaker, Certified in Creating Champion Conversation Public Speaking and now an Author. She is a Member of Mechanicsville United Methodist Church where she serves as Lay Leader. She is a lover of God and mankind. Sandra has a passion for people and desires to see people mentally well and win in life.

She describes herself as a People Builder as some

people build houses she builds people. She believes that we are to heal and go out and heal someone else. She describes herself as Wounded Healer and Overcomer. She loves Dr. Maya Angelou quote: "When We Get Give! When We Learn Teach! For we can never hold on to life all we can do is give it away! "

She enjoys reading, watching action and faith based movies, traveling and meeting new people and writing. She is Employed at Pee Dee Mental Health as an Adult Services Counselor.

Contact Information:

Sandra Gamble

Facebook: https://www.facebook.com/sandra.gamble.5

Email: gamble11535@msn.com

Cashapp: $SanCorey

* 9 7 9 8 6 8 1 5 0 0 2 3 0 *